Montana

A PHOTOGRAPHIC CELEBRA

VOLUME 3

Text by A.B. Guthrie, Jr.
Photography compiled by Rick Graetz
Photo editing by Susie Beaulaurier Graetz

Published by Rick Graetz
Northern Rockies Publishing Company
through Montana Magazine, Helena, Montana

Introduction

HOWARD SKAGGS PHOTO
COURTESY UNIVERSITY OF MONTANA

BILL KINNEY

A.B. Guthrie, Jr.
January 13, 1901—April 26, 1991

This past spring Montana lost one of its giants, when A.B. (Bud) Guthrie, Jr. passed from the earth. And this writer lost a friend and hero. The name Bud Guthrie is best known to most Montanans as that of a great writer, author of *The Big Sky* and Pulitzer Prize winner. To many of us, however, he will also be remembered as a progressive voice from Montana and spiritual spokesman for the Rocky Mountain Front. He lent his considerable reputation to conservation efforts. His insights regarding Montana and the west, its development and its fragility added muscle to the cause—for here was a man of hefty writing accomplishments, nationally known and attuned to Montana's historic and continuing role as a victim to outside interests and inside greed. His honest observations marked by clarity of expression illuminated Montana's social and environmental dilemmas and turned the tables on those who would have it all, fast, now. Guthrie said what the heart knows: this land and its wild things are all we've got. In his words:

"There are too many among us who think first and only of the immediate personal profit, not of the long-term and irreparable loss. They'll figure that posterity never did anything for them and to hell with it." Or, offering hope: "Not everything is lost. The air around my old home is still clean and tonic; Ear Mountain still stands and I imagine industrious boys still can find fish, and in the fall see a cottontail sitting. Boys can still dream their boys' dreams...I would preserve what remains of these old riches. I would save these encouragements, these fulfillments, these opportunities for those who will be me again. Posterity owes us nothing. The truth is quite different. We owe a good world to posterity."

And, about Montana, he said: "I love Montana. She is home to me, the center of my universe, a mighty and wonderful world, and I pray against the forces that would destroy her."

Bud Guthrie wrote and fought for the land up until the day of his death. He was encouraged and inspired by his wife, Carol.

We will miss Bud Guthrie. This, the third volume in the Montana Photographic Celebration series, is dedicated to this great man. And, Bud, we will do our best to carry on your good work.

Rick Graetz
Bigfork, Montana
July 1991

KRISTI DuBOIS

ISBN 1-56037-007-6
All typesetting, design and pre-press production completed in the U.S.A.
Northern Rockies Publishing Company, Helena, MT
Printed in Hong Kong

Montana Magazine staff
photographers use Kodak film

Rick Graetz

President of American & World Geographic Publishing, and publisher of *Montana Magazine*, Rick Graetz is a photojournalist, environmentalist, civic and political activist. He is the author of *Cuba: The Land, The People, Havana: The City, The People,* and *Vietnam: Opening Doors to the World,* published by American Geographic. Through his private imprint, Northern Rockies Publishing, he has in recent years authored two editions of *Montana: A Photographic Celebration, Montana Is,* and *Montana's Bob Marshall Country.* Graetz is also part owner of and guide for High Country Adventures, a backpacking and mountaineering outfitting service. He has photographed, climbed and skied mountains and floated rivers throughout North America, South America, Hawaii and Asia.

Left: *Badlands along the Powder River south of Miles City.*
Above: *Southern Bitterroot Valley and Como Peak.*
Above left: *Mule deer.*

Title page: *Bull elk.* DONALD M. JONES

Front cover: *Early morning in the al-pine country of the Beartooth Moun-tains, Shoshone National Forest.* GREG RYAN/SALLY BEYER

Back cover, clockwise from top right:
Evening grosbeak. MARK LAGERSTROM
Beating the heat on Flathead Lake. RICK AND SUSIE GRAETZ
Snowshoe hare. ALAN AND SANDY CAREY
Seeing the sights in an open-top tour bus on Going-to-the-Sun Road, Glacier National Park. GREG RYAN/SALLY BEYER
End of a pheasant hunting day. ALAN AND SANDY CAREY
Young ice fisherman at Savage Lake. DONALD M. JONES

Above: *The Swan Range.*

Facing page: *Chalk Buttes in eastern Montana.*

Right: *Ninepipe Reservoir near Charlo.*

Below: *Common loon.*

The subject today is the Front, the great Rocky Mountain Front in which I live. The question is how to preserve it and its values. I wish I knew a way. Of one thing I am sure. It is expressed in an old quatrain, so old it has no attribution. It goes this way:

The law locks up the man or woman
Who steals the goose from off the common,
But lets the greater felon loose
Who steals the common from the goose.

Unless we are vigilant, the Front will be stolen from us geese.

You will find a great deal of poetry in the rest of what I have to say. I believe that allusion is more effective than open declaration. And poetry is a suggester, not a declarer.

I have spent time and energy, especially in these latter years, informing, alerting, and haranguing people to the dangers of losing our natural inheritance. The Front is unique. Its peril is real. Solutions are hard to find. To use an old Western expression, I'm reaching the end of my rope. But I shall never stop caring. Today I put the job in your fresher, stronger hands.

Fight for the Front, you younger folk. Find the answers.

Sawtooth Ridge, Rocky Mountain Front.

RICK GRAETZ

Above: *"Snow ghosts" in Yellowstone National Park.*
Left: *Wolf.*

Facing page: *11,300-foot Hilgard Peak in the Lee Metcalf Wilderness Area.*

Above: *White rocks area along the Wild and Scenic Missouri River.*
Right: *Tabletop rocks, Missouri River.*

Facing page: *Upper Missouri River at La Barge Rock.*

ROBERT C. GILDART

Left: *View of Desolation Peak from Two Medicine Pass, Glacier National Park.*
Above: *Spanish Peaks.*

Above: *Sunrise, Lee Metcalf Refuge.*
Right: *Heading home after a hard day's work.*

Facing page: *Rainbow near Wilsall.*

WAYNE MUMFORD

Montana

This land is mine,
Or I am its.
I curse the cold,
The always wind,
The sun's glare in July.
I vow to leave,
But know I won't,
Remembering…
The shimmer of high plains,
The sky-cut of the heights,
Buck's antlers through a leaf-screen,
Trout lipping beaver ponds.
Warm days follow cold.
Soft winds follow hard.
Clouds come to filter glare.
At six o'clock or thereabouts
The hour of no wind falls.
The aspen leaves find rest,
And time is harmony.
Montana begs forgiveness
For its caprice
And I forgive.

*The Continental Divide in Gla-
cier National Park.*

JAMES W. POWER

DAVID MATHERLY

Left: *Springtime east of Joliet.*
Below: *Big Snowy Mountains in central Montana.*

Facing page: *Mt. Black, Absaroka Mountains.*

Above: *Lupine and arrowleaf balsamroot in Cottonwood Canyon, Gallatin National Forest.*
Right: *Bitterroot, the Montana state flower.*

Left: *Babysitting, Canada goose style.*
Below: *Red Rock River and the Centennial Mountains.*

I am not fixed in opposition to all change. The conditions of life leave vast room for improvement, but change, proposed change, man-managed change, needs consideration, not haste. Blind change leaves sores and regrets, no matter that it marches under the bright banner of progress...the fact to be kept first in mind, is that we in Montana have invaded the gifts we inherited. We have drawn on our principal. We have lived off it. We have sold off...what can't be re-

Above: Lonesome Mountain in the Beartooth Wilderness.

Facing page: Ennis Lake and the Madison Range.

Mixed Chorus

On frosty nights of autumn
and frosty nights of spring
I hear the wild geese shouting
and hear coyotes sing.

Sad voices from the hills,
stout voices from the sky,
grief and cheers and wild things—
one blood, they and I.

*Emigrant Peak in the Paradise
Valley.*

27

DENNIS J. CWIDAK

DEL SIEGLE

Above: *Wildflowers in the Spanish Peaks.*
Right: *Sagebrush and snowdrifts near Glendive.*

Facing page: *Palisade Falls, Gallatin National Forest.*

KRISTI DuBOIS

Right: Lake Mc-
Donald, Glacier
National Park.
Below: American
avocets, Benton
Lake National
Wildlife Refuge
near Great Falls.

Left: Clouds over "The Silos" at Canyon Ferry Lake.
Below: Great North Mountain and Stanton Lake in the Great Bear Wilderness.

Facing page: Madison Range, Lee Metcalf Wilderness.

Introduction to fishing journal kept by my family, who love to fish the Teton.

Old days, and the Teton flows bright, and the water is an inviting blue-green at the bends, where the current has scoured holes, and trout lie waiting.

We are three, our father, my young brother and I. Our horse, unhitched from the buggy, stands tied to a tree in the shade. We are putting our jointed rods together and stringing lines from the reels, and Chickie's little-boy voice tells us, "I smell fish."

My father and I smile at each other, knowing he doesn't. But did he? did he? Over the years, over seventy-odd of them, I hear his eager voice, and I smell fish, too.

There's the fly book with its beautiful lures, all named by poets when fishing was poetry. What will we choose? The Royal Coachman? The King or the Queen of Waters? Or something else? Maybe the Grizzly King, or the Professor, or the Silver Doctor, or the Ginger Quill or the Parmacheene Belle.

Then to fishing that lovely stream, just right in size, big enough for casting, safe enough to wade, and at noon our father halts on a gravel bank, saying the creel is getting heavy, and how about some lunch? We open a box of crackers and, fitting for the occasion, cans of sardines.

And here, on this chosen bank with the sun bright on the pebbles, here is the world's choicest spot, here is God's privacy, here the best moment the earth has to offer.

Old days, old joys, and Father joshing with us, and Chickie's voice in my ears, and the Teton flowing.

KIM & KARI BAKER

Above: Early morning trout fishing in southwest Montana.

Facing page: Summer's leftovers.

Right: *A field of gold in Gallatin County.*
Below: *Farmland near Babb.*

Facing page: *The statehood-centennial wagon train near Montana City.*

DAN WAGGONER

Above: Beargrass and the Chinese Wall, Bob Marshall Wilderness.

Facing page: Cinnamon black bear.

Above: Rock Creek Canyon in the Beartooth Mountains near Red Lodge.

Facing page, top: Rough Lake at dusk, Beartooth Mountains.
Bottom: Crazy Mountains.

JOHN REDDY

RICK GRAETZ

41

The history of Montana and the story of the Indian in the state are so mixed as sometimes to seem almost the same. A quick look around is enough. The designated battle sites, the towns established because of the presence of Indians or because of trade or fear of attack, real or imagined, testify to that association. Kalispell, Fort Benton and Miles City are three examples.

The reservations scattered over the state are added proof.

Indians have retained or renewed old customs in the form of celebrations, powwows and re-enactments of historical events.

The Indian is no longer ashamed of being Indian, as the young fellows were once made to feel.

Thank the Lord…The Indian has recovered his pride of race. He had no good reason to be ashamed anyhow. His cause was just, though he met defeat.

In the course of history, many a just cause becomes a lost cause.

ALAN & SANDY CAREY

MICHAEL CRUMMETT

43

MICHAEL S. QUINTON

Left: *Mountain goat.*
Below: *A ground blizzard near East Glacier.*

Facing page: *St. Mary's Lake and Goose Island, Glacier National Park.*

45

WAYNE MUMFORD

Above: *Mission Mountains.*
Left: *Tobacco Root Mountains.*

Left: *The horse outlasted the car.*
Below: *Lower Yellowstone River near Glendive.*

Facing page: *Southeastern Montana.*

CHARLES E. KAY

Above: Beargrass.
Left: Blue Paradise Lake, Hilgard Basin.

Right: *Mountain sheep in the Many Glacier Valley, Glacier National Park.*
Below: *Mt. Harding of the Mission Range.*

Facing page: *A cozy winter retreat.*

RICK GRAETZ

In spite of the vagaries of the weather and the ups and downs of the markets for livestock and grains Montana cities and towns remain pretty stable. That's all to the good. In place of striving for industrialization and growth, that's what I think the state and its localities should keep in mind—stability. It's a lot better than boom and bust. Years ago Alexander Pope wrote, "To stay where you are is somewhat to advance."

MICHAEL CRUMMETT

Above: Montana Centennial Wagon Train
participant Merle Curtis.
Left: Along the Skalkaho Highway.

Above: *The Bighole River near Wisdom.*

Facing page, top: *Pronghorn doe and fawns.*
Bottom: *Bighorn Lake.*

Above: Rainbow Lake in the Beartooth Mountains lake plateau country.
Right: Bighole Valley near Jackson.

Facing page: Waiting for a rider at the bucking horse sale in Miles City.

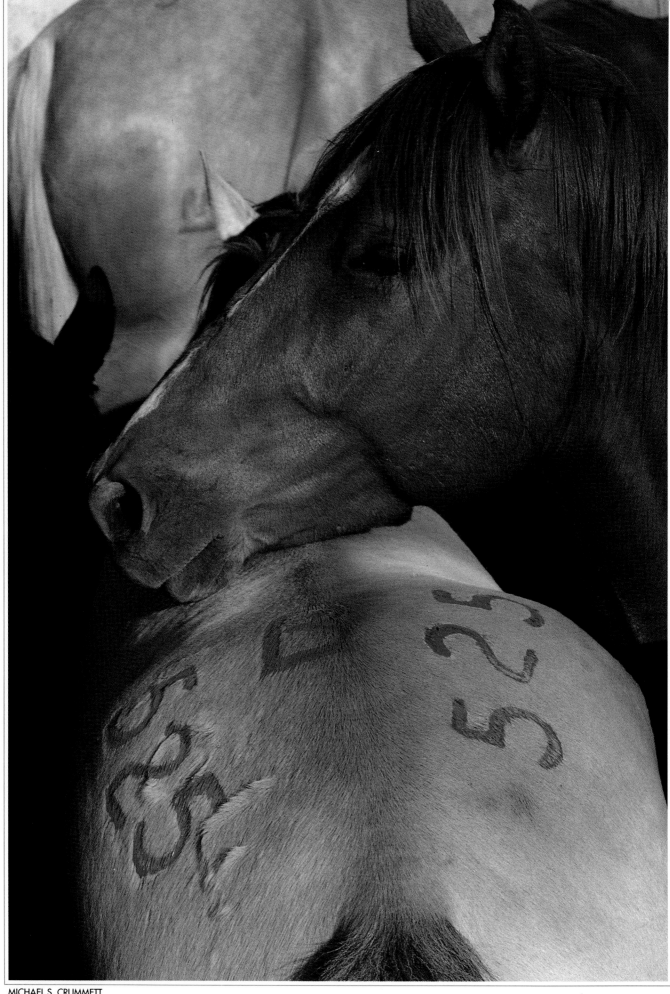

MICHAEL S. CRUMMETT

59

Above: *The fragile country of the Hilgard Basin.*

Facing page: *The Questa sails Flathead Lake.*

The pen being said to be mightier than the sword, one might hope that it would also be equal to a passel of politicians, or to public indifference.

It is the philosophers, the thinkers, who by their words and actions have directed our destiny. I am thinking of Jefferson and Lincoln and others who formulated our ideals by their words and deeds and made us the nation we are.

A man or woman who cares about preserving our land for future generations will reflect that in his or her work. A writer, expressing his perceptions, can, in turn, strike an answering recognition in the mind of the reader—or cause an awakening to something never thought of before.

One doesn't do this through boring tirades or gratuitous moralizing, but through the honesty or conviction of his or her own thoughts or vision.

Reading of a countryside, loved and cherished by a character, can forever change a reader's perceptions. One moment, perfectly crystallized, can become a part of a reader.

But beware. I once wrote a rather lyrical piece about trout fishing in our state. It resulted in a flood of letters, all asking if I couldn't direct them to a cabin site by the banks of a good trout stream. I hardly need to tell you it wasn't my purpose to bring more people here.

Just remember—if you care enough, that caring will surface in your writing. Who knows what fires you may light?

RICK GRAETZ

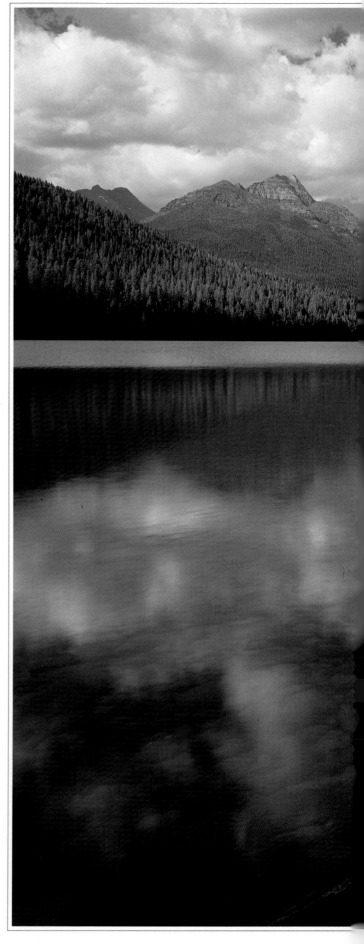

Above: *Jones columbine.*
Right: *Bowman Lake, Glacier National Park.*

Above: *A misty morning in the Madison Range.*
Left: *South Moccasin Mountains at Glengarry.*

Facing page: *The view from Mt. James, Glacier National Park.*

TOM DIETRICH

I am a resident, you might almost say a product, of the Rocky Mountain Front, "the Front" as we have come to call it. It is a strip of land just east of the Continental Divide and includes an edge of the plains, the higher benchlands, the foothills and then the great jagged wall of the mountains.

At the age of 89, living on the Front, I have come to feel a part of what has gone before, kin to dinosaur and buffalo and departed Indians that lived here. When I step out of doors and hear a small crunch underfoot I sometimes suspect I may be treading on the dusted bones of duckbill or bison or red man killed in the hunt.

I look to the north and the south, where the foothills rise, east to the great jagged roll of the high plains and west to the mountains and my vision site of Ear Mountain, and good medicine lies all around.

The Rocky Mountain Front near Augusta.

Right: *Thistle championship race on Flathead Lake.*
Below: *A Christmas tree farm near Kalispell.*

Facing page: *Apple blossoms in the Flathead Valley near Creston.*

DOUG DYE

Above: *Stony Indian Pass country in Glacier National Park.*
Right: *Clark Canyon Reservoir south of Dillon.*

Above: *Sieben Flat near Wolf Creek Canyon.*
Right: *Historic Marysville.*

Facing page: *Farrier Rock Dresen with the first customer of the day.*

Above: *Coming through East Glacier.*
Right: *The Big Hole Valley.*

Above: *Lower Aero Lake in the Beartooth Mountains.*
Right: *Beartrap Canyon Road, Tobacco Root Range.*

Facing page: *White-tailed ptarmigan.*

Ear Mountain

Ear Mountain stands four miles away,
crow-flight, from our house.
No day passes but I gaze on it
as my father did when I was young.
I see him looking out the window west,
His eyes fixed and his body still.
Restive, he found peace there perhaps,
or in it some continuation of himself,
some promise of foreverness.
I did not know his thoughts,
nor am I clear about my own
as its lift invites my eye,
and somehow I am part of it,
a mortal partner to eternity.

Ear Mountain itself.

RICK GRAETZ

Left: *Pentagon Mountain and Dean Lake.*
Below: *In the Medicine Rocks area.*

Facing page: *Farmland as seen from "The Knees" in north-central Montana.*

CHRISTIAN HEEB

Above: Fireweed flowers below Granite Peak.

Facing page, top: The top of Prairie Reef, looking toward the Chinese Wall.
Bottom: Strawberry Creek Outfitters crossing the Continental Divide in the Bob Marshall Wilderness.

ED WOLFF

Above: Moose and calf.
Right: Autumn in the Mission Valley.

MARTY SHIELDS

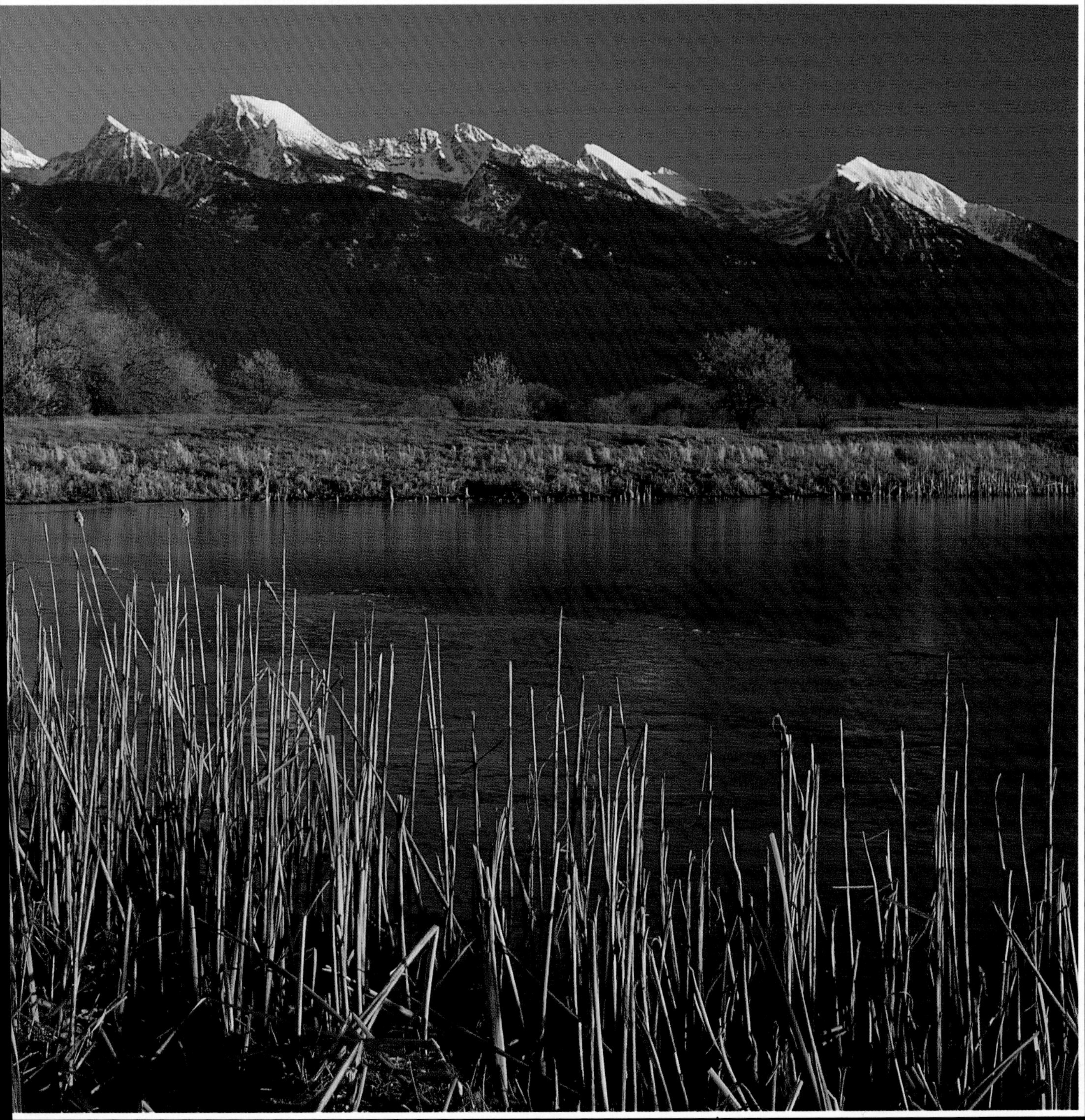

Right: Mountain lion cub.
Below: Rainbow Lakes, Beartooth lake plateau country.

Facing page: Mt. Cowan as seen from Mt. Black in the Absarokas.

DAVID MATHERLY

I t was on an early cold day of spring that we found a horned lark drooping on our back stoop. He just stood there, perhaps too sick to be afraid, when we opened the door. A small, forlorn creature, victim of the world's cruelties.

In early spring horned larks appear by the hundreds along Montana's roadsides, and what if your car hits one? No big deal. There are plenty more.

But it became important to my wife and me that this small, sad specimen live. We brought it in, put it on a paper, kept it warm and scattered bird seed for it. Two days later it had recovered. We took it out gently and let it take wing, wishing it well.

There's a moral or lesson or illustration here, but I won't take over the pulpit, no matter the temptation.

The Judith River Valley near the Missouri River.

Above: Louise Lake, Tobacco Root Mountains.

Facing page: A two-week-old mule deer fawn.

Right: Echo Lake in the Flathead Valley.
Below: Out-buildings east of Norris.

Facing page: The view from Reno-Ben-teen Battlefield near Crow Agency.

Above: From the top of Lonesome Peak in the
Beartooth Wilderness.

Facing page: Seeing double: a mated pair of
bald eagles.

Right: *West of Billings.*
Below: *"The Knees" in north-central Montana.*

Facing page: *Trapper Peak, Bitterroot Mountains.*

MARK LAGERSTROM

There are advantages to living in a small town—and most Montana towns are small. You know the owners of the groceries and hardware stores, the proprietors of eating places, the mayor and commissioners, the servants of government, the electricians, the plumbers, the lawyers. So, if anything goes wrong or questions arise, you know to whom to go—not to some unidentified clerk serving a line-up or secretary asking if you have an appointment, but to a friend or acquaintance who owns the place that serves the public interest.

Go to the butcher and say the steak you bought was too tough to eat, and he'll say sorry, here try this one. Go to the hardware store to complain, and the man or woman there will be sympathetic and offer a new product in exchange, or ask do you want your money back?

So, in thinking about the advantages of the big cities, think of the advantages not to be found.

MICHAEL CRUMMETT

Above: Wilsall.
Left: Sam's Supper
Club in Glasgow.

Facing page: Rodeo
parade in Lincoln.

Above: *Beauty and the beast: spring setting for a grizzly bear.*

Facing page, top: *Spanish Peaks Primitive Area.*
Bottom: *Rainey Lake.*

ROB OUTLAW

LARRY JAVORSKY

Right: An old barn in central Montana.
Below: Winter cattle drive by Grasshopper Creek in the Pioneer Mountains.

Facing page: Crazy Mountains south of Martinsdale.

Overleaf: Bull elk.

I s our self-importance, if not our need, so great as to justify decisions
and practices that will deprive and impoverish generations to come?
By what right do we consume and exhaust what can't be replaced? No
one really owns land or resources. We use it under trusteeship, and the
good trustee conserves and even improves what has been given to him to
protect. A look to the future goes beyond anyone's lifetime.

MICHAEL QUINTON